Maps Are Flat,
Globes Are Round

Meg Greve

ROURKE PUBLISHING

Vero Beach, Florida 32964

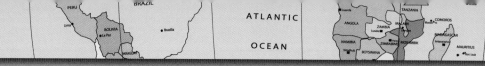

www.rourkepublishing.com

PHOTO CREDITS: © Slobo Mitic: Title Page, 18, 23; © Maria Zhuravleva: Title Page, 7, 22, 23; © Carmen MartÃnez BanÃ°s; © Marc Lantrok: 4, © MACIEJ NOSKOWSKI: 5; © suemack: 5; © iofoto: 9; © Valerie Loiseleux: 11; © exi5: 13, 19; © Jan Tyler: 14; © Carmen Martínez Banús: 15, 22; © lara seregni: 16; © Martin Strmko: 17, 22, 23; © Sergiy Zavgorodny: 21

Edited by Jeanne Sturm

Cover design by Nicola Stratford bppublishing.com
Interior design by Renee Brady

Library of Congress Cataloging-in-Publication Data

Greve, Meg.
  Maps are flat, globes are round / Meg Greve.
     p. cm. -- (Little world geography)
  Includes bibliographical references and index.
  ISBN 978-1-60694-417-2 (Hardcover)
  ISBN 978-1-60694-533-9 (Softcover)
  1. Maps--Juvenile literature. 2. Globes--Juvenile literature. I. Title.
  GA105.6.G74 2010
  912--dc22
                              2009006019

Printed in the USA

CG/CG

ROURKE PUBLISHING

www.rourkepublishing.com - rourke@rourkepublishing.com
Post Office Box 643328 Vero Beach, Florida 32964

A **map** is flat.

A map has colors like green or blue.

A map always gives us a bird's eye view.

A **globe** is round, so it sits on a **stand**.

Turn it around to see **oceans** and land.

There are many different types of maps: big ones and little ones, just for our laps.

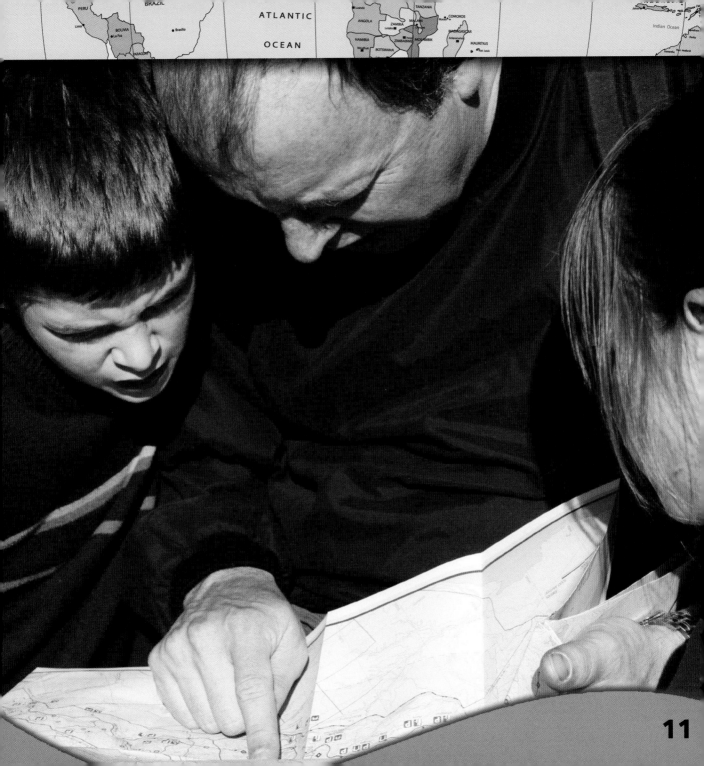

Street maps show us where to drive cars.

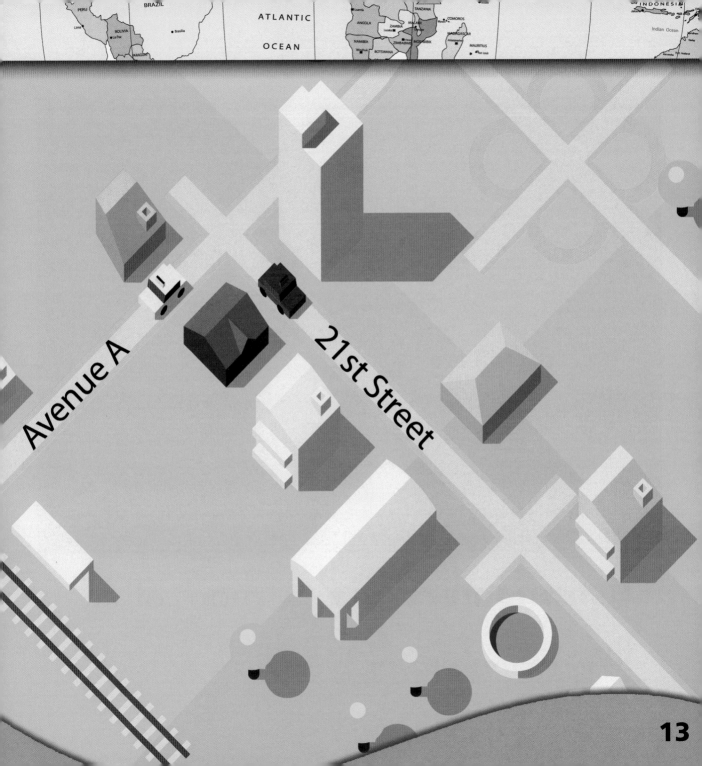

Avenue A

21st Street

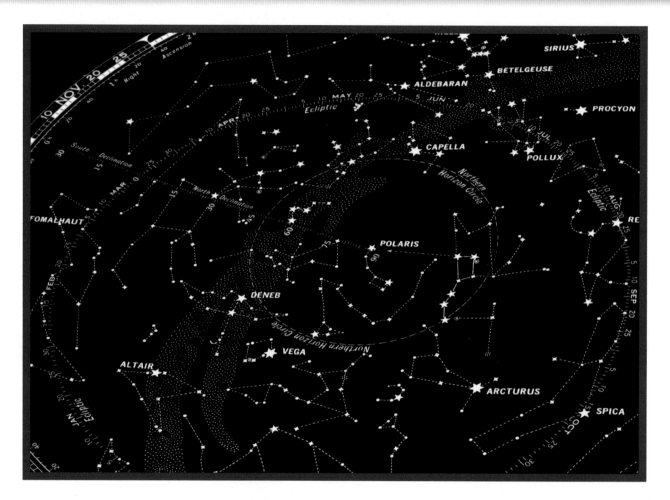

Astronomers use a map of
the stars.

Divers use maps to explore the ocean floor.

You might use one to find
a toy store.

Toy Store

Avenue A

21st Street

If you like to hike, walk, or roam, a map or globe will get you home.

GLOSSARY

astronomers (uh-STRON-uh-muhrz): Astronomers are people who study objects in outer space. Astronomers use maps of the stars, telescopes, and computers to study the universe.

divers (DYE-vurs): Divers are people who swim down into deep water. They have to wear special equipment that lets them breathe under water.

globe (GLOHB): A globe is a sphere or ball-shaped model with a map of the Earth printed on it. Globes usually show larger areas of land and water, such as continents and oceans.

map (MAP): A map is a drawing that shows where things are, such as towns, roads, rivers, or mountains. People use maps when they need to know how to get somewhere.

oceans (OH-shuhns): Oceans are the largest bodies of water on Earth. The water is salty. There are five major oceans: the Pacific, Atlantic, Indian, Arctic, and Southern.

stand (STAND): A stand holds a globe in place to keep it from rolling. Sometimes the globe is stuck on the stand. Sometimes you can take the globe off the stand.

Index

Websites to Visit

www.funbrain.com

www.enchantedlearning.com/usa/states

www.maps4kids.com

www.fedstats.gov/kids/mapstats

kids.nationalgeographic.com

About the Author

Meg Greve lives in Chicago with her husband, daughter, and son. She loves to study maps and imagines traveling to new and different places.